MOONDIAL

In the garden of Belton House stands a sundial, but the shadow that falls on it at night comes from moonlight, not sunlight. And a moondial tells a different kind of time.

Minty Cane has a sixth sense – a sense which understands things that cannot be seen or heard by other people. When she first enters the garden at Belton House, she knows at once that there is some mystery waiting for her . . . and the moondial is at the heart of the mystery.

Soon the moondial takes Minty travelling, to the same garden a hundred years ago. There she meets Tom, a poor servant boy with a painful cough. And then the moondial sends her even further back to another century, where she hears a child's sad voice singing in the moonlit garden . . .

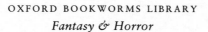

OXFORD BOOKWORMS LIBRARY
Fantasy & Horror

Moondial

Stage 3 (1000 headwords)

Series Editor: Jennifer Bassett
Founder Editor: Tricia Hedge
Activities Editors: Jennifer Bassett and Christine Lindop

HELEN CRESSWELL

Moondial

Retold by
John Escott

Illustrated by
Gerry Grace

OXFORD UNIVERSITY PRESS
2000

Oxford University Press
Great Clarendon Street, Oxford OX2 6DP

Oxford New York

Athens Auckland Bangkok Bogotá Buenos Aires Calcutta Cape Town
Chennai Dar es Salaam Delhi Florence Hong Kong Istanbul Karachi
Kuala Lumpur Madrid Melbourne Mexico City Mumbai Nairobi
Paris São Paulo Singapore Taipei Tokyo Toronto Warsaw
and associated companies in
Berlin Ibadan

OXFORD and OXFORD ENGLISH
are trade marks of Oxford University Press

ISBN 0 19 423009 0

Original edition © Helen Cresswell 1987
First published by Faber and Faber Limited 1987
This simplified edition © Oxford University Press 2000

First published in Oxford Bookworms 1996
This second edition published in the Oxford Bookworms Library 2000

Typeset by Wyvern Typesetting Ltd, Bristol

Printed in Spain

CONTENTS

STORY INTRODUCTION   i

It is midnight . . .   1
1 More than shadows   2
2 The sundial   8
3 Children from the past   16
4 Devil's child!   24
5 Miss Vole   32
6 'Someone walking over my grave . . .'   42
7 The end of the game   47

GLOSSARY   58
ACTIVITIES: Before Reading   60
ACTIVITIES: While Reading   61
ACTIVITIES: After Reading   64
ABOUT THE AUTHOR   68
ABOUT BOOKWORMS   69

IT IS MIDNIGHT in that most dark and secret place. You can hear the cry of a bird from the top of the church, and smell the old yew trees. You put out a hand – and touch cold stone. The shock brings a fear that you can almost taste. Now a slow silver light comes over the garden. Statues appear. You notice the shadow that the moon has made at your feet, and you stand very still.

You can see, hear, taste, smell, touch . . . and perhaps something more. And if you have that sixth sense, what then? First a cold feeling, like a finger down your back; then a sudden shaking, all through you. You look up at a statue – a big stone man, and a small boy. Suddenly, you are *sure* that there are eyes watching you.

You turn slowly and look at the empty windows of the great moonlit house. Then the moon goes back behind the clouds – and you run! And as you run, you hear strange, frightened voices. What you also hear – and will remember always – is the lonely crying of a child.

— 1 —
More than shadows

Minty Cane had known she was a witch, or something like it, since she was small. She had woken at night to see shadowy people moving silently across the floor of her room, or heard invisible feet. She did not talk about these things because she did not think them strange. She had once spoken of a dark visitor to her mother, Kate, but Kate had talked about lights from cars in the street making shadows. In the past year, Minty sometimes heard her father's voice. And she knew that *was* strange, because he was dead.

Kate worked all day at the hospital, so for the summer holidays she decided that Minty should go to the village of Belton and stay with an old friend of Kate's family. Aunt Mary lived in a little stone house opposite Belton House, which was large and beautiful and once belonged to Lord Brownlow. None of the Brownlow family lived there now and the house was open to visitors from April to October.

'I always think of Belton as a place where things *happen*,' said Kate. 'When I was small and stayed with Aunt Mary, I had the front bedroom. I could see the top of the church, and bits of the garden at Belton House.'

'Were there ghosts?' said Minty.

Suddenly Minty felt cold air pass over her.

'Perhaps. But I never actually *saw* anything.'

They drove to Belton the day after school finished, and Aunt Mary was waiting at her front door.

'You've grown,' she told Minty, then said to Kate, 'She'll have the same room that you always had.'

They went upstairs and Kate helped Minty to unpack her suitcase. Then they came down for the lunch that Aunt Mary had cooked for them. After lunch Kate and Minty went to look at the church, which was only a short walk away. The July afternoon was hot and still, and they walked slowly through the churchyard, stopping to read gravestones as they passed.

Suddenly Minty felt cold air pass over her face and arms. She was near a corner of the church and she looked up at the trees, but there was no wind in them. She took a few steps forward, and the coldness came with her. And then the air was warm again, and quiet.

'Now that,' thought Minty, 'is very strange.'

She stepped back to the corner and felt the invisible icy wind again – and her sixth sense told her there was something more. The ice-cold air was only a message, and she stood still, listening, waiting.

Then Kate came up beside Minty. 'Do you feel cold?' Minty asked her. 'Just *here*, in this place?'

'Mmmm.' Kate did suddenly put her arms around herself. 'It's the shadows, I suppose.'

'More than shadows,' thought Minty.

They went into the church and it was cool and dark after the brightness outside. After looking round, they came out into the sun and looked across at a high gate. Behind it were the gardens of Belton House. The air smelled hundreds of years old and Minty suddenly felt that time was standing still. 'If time *has* stopped,' she thought, 'here among the gravestones is the right place. They're all dead, and it doesn't matter if you died yesterday or a hundred years ago. Dead is dead.'

Later, Kate drove away in her little car, then Minty went to her room to listen to some music on her cassette player. Kate didn't think Aunt Mary would like pop music so she had bought Minty some headphones to use.

Minty was still listening when Aunt Mary called her for tea. They went downstairs, and the telephone rang. 'You start your tea,' said Aunt Mary, and went to answer it.

Minty went to her room to listen to some music.

5

Minty was eating her second egg sandwich when Aunt Mary came back. Her face was very white and her eyes looked wild and shocked. 'I don't know how to—' She stopped, then went on, 'It's Kate – your mother! There's been an accident. Her head . . .'

It was then that Minty began to scream.

It had been a bad crash on a busy road. Kate's car had been between two other cars, and now she was in hospital. Minty was back in her room when the telephone rang again. She was feeling cold and sick, and several minutes later Aunt Mary brought in a cup of hot, sweet tea.

'That was someone called John,' she said. 'Mr Benson. From your mother's office.'

Minty knew him. He came to the house sometimes and played computer games with her, and made her laugh.

'He's going to the hospital now,' said Aunt Mary.

'I want to go!' said Minty. 'Can I?'

'Tomorrow,' said Aunt Mary. 'Perhaps she'll be awake by then. It's her head, you see . . . it was badly hurt.'

Minty knew that if her mother was in a coma, it could last a long time. She did not believe Kate would be awake in the morning. 'Can I go outside?' she asked. 'I must do something!'

'Go over to the House, then. See if World is there, at the lodge. He likes children.'

'World?' said Minty.

An old man was sitting near the entrance.

'*Mr* World to you, I suppose,' said Aunt Mary.

So Minty went out. A bus full of school-children was leaving the House. Some of them smiled at her through the bus windows, and Minty automatically smiled back. An old man was sitting in the doorway of a stone building near the entrance. 'This must be World,' Minty thought.

'Hello,' he said. 'Did you miss the bus?'

7

'No, I'm staying with Aunt Mary, over the road.'

'Oh, yes, I heard,' he said. 'What's your name?'

Minty told him. 'It's short for Araminta.'

'An unusual name for an unusual person,' he said. 'Am I right? You've come to meet the children, haven't you?'

'Are there children living in the House?' she said, surprised.

'I didn't say anything about *living*.' He spoke quietly and watched her carefully.

'You mean . . . ghosts?' she said.

'I didn't *say* that. But when I saw you, I thought, "That's the one to let those children free!" I hear their voices in the wind. They're asking me to help them, but I can't do anything. But now you've come.'

'Yes,' said Minty. 'I've come.'

She did not really understand what the old man was saying, but she knew for sure that something strange, and perhaps dangerous, was waiting for her.

– 2 –

The sundial

'Mr Benson will take us to the hospital this afternoon,' Aunt Mary told her at breakfast the next morning. 'Your mother is still not – not awake, but she's comfortable.'

Minty had to get out again, so she went to look at the House and gardens after breakfast. She saw the silvery-blue roof of the House and the entrance to a courtyard beyond. The courtyard was empty. There was a clock on the roof of a low building. It had a blue face and showed the wrong time. On the other side of the courtyard there was a door, half-open. Minty walked across and went through. There was another door beyond, and she passed between cold stone walls and gave the door a push.

The courtyard was empty.

'The garden!' she said.

It was quiet in the early sun. There were paths, grass, yew trees and statues, and Minty knew at once that this garden was waiting for her. She walked down seven steps to a path that went to the centre of the garden.

Immediately, she was sure that someone was watching her. She turned, but no one was there, and there were no faces at the windows of the House. She walked on towards a statue that stood in the centre where the paths crossed, and as she stopped in front of it, she felt the air around her turn icy cold.

The statue was of a boy and an old man. They seemed to be fighting to hold a bowl above their heads. Minty suddenly realized what it was.

'The garden!' she said.

10

'A sundial!' she said softly, and then, without knowing why – 'Moondial!' As she spoke the word, a cold wind went past her, and her ears were filled with a thousand frightened voices. She shut her eyes and put her hands over her ears – and the voices and the wind went away. Minty opened her eyes . . . *and knew she was in a different morning, not the one that she had woken up to.*

The garden seemed smaller. She looked at the House and saw smoke coming from a chimney where there had been no smoke before. She began to run to the courtyard and almost ran into a boy. 'Sorry!' she said.

The boy jumped back and looked at her. 'Oh!' he said. His eyes were large and frightened in his thin white face. 'I've never seen one that *talked* before!'

Minty looked at his strange coat and trousers and knew she was seeing what most people called a ghost.

'I'll shut my eyes,' the boy said to himself. 'Then, when I open them, she'll be gone.'

'*I* will, too!' said Minty.

They both closed their eyes, then opened them again.

'We haven't disappeared,' he laughed.

'No,' agreed Minty.

'I've seen ghosts before,' he said.

'But – but *you're* the ghost!' said Minty.

He laughed again. 'Oh, yes? Then why did Cook tell me to run and get some vegetables for dinner?' He began to move away. 'I can't stand here talking all day.'

'Wait!' said Minty. 'Let's shake hands!'

11

'Why?' he said.

'Because one of us won't be able to, not if we're a ghost,' she said. 'Ghosts go *through* things.'

He thought for a moment, then he put out his hand. Minty took it in hers. Warm hand met warm hand.

'We're both real!' Minty said softly. 'What's your name?'

'Tom,' he said. 'Short for Edward.'

She laughed. 'I'm Minty. Short for Penelope.'

'What do you do? Do you work downstairs, too?'

'What do *you* do?' she asked, not sure what to say.

'Everything. Fetch and carry. Clean the floors. They haven't decided yet. I'm from London, and I want to be a footman. But footmen have to be tall, you see, so I've got to grow a bit first.'

Warm hand met warm hand.

'How old are you?' asked Minty.

'Don't know. About twelve, I suppose,' he answered.

'Why don't you ask your mother?' she said.

'Dead,' he said. 'And my father. I've got brothers and sisters in London, but I never see them. I miss little Dorrie. She's seven or eight, and when I'm a footman I'll bring her here.' He pulled his thin body up straight and tall, but then began to cough painfully, a hard, dry sound.

There was a sudden shout. 'Here – boy!'

Minty saw a man. A gardener, she guessed. 'Are you coming for those vegetables, or aren't you?' he shouted.

'I'm coming – I'm coming now, sir,' said Tom.

Tom went and Minty watched. The man began to speak, and between each word he hit Tom hard on the head.

'New from London, aren't you. *Boys* from *London* must *do* what they're *told*!'

Tom covered his head with his arms and Minty ran to him. 'Stop it!' she screamed. She began to hit the man and – 'Oh!' She found herself hitting the empty air! The man and Tom had disappeared!

Minty looked around her . . . and saw that the morning had changed again. She did not need to lift her eyes to know that the smoke had gone from the chimney.

'What happened?' she wondered. 'What did I do to make time jump? What did I do to go back all those years? A hundred, at least . . .'

She looked at the centre of the garden and remembered. The sundial . . . moondial . . .

She walked back to it and touched it again. But this time nothing happened. No icy wind, no voices.

'But I *will* get back,' she said. 'You'll see!'

Minty sat in the back of Mr Benson's car, on the way to the hospital. Mr Benson was trying to explain to her.

'Your mother,' he began.

'She's asleep,' said Aunt Mary.

'No, it's more than that,' said Mr Benson. 'But you mustn't be frightened, Minty. She's still *there*, and she'll

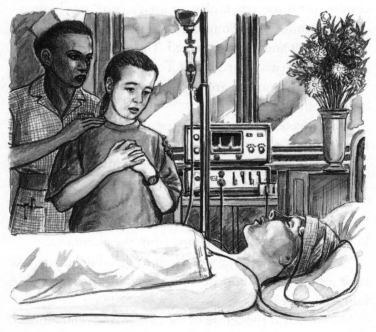

'Hello, Kate . . . Mum . . .'

14

know that *you're* there, too.'

'Please let her eyes be open,' thought Minty.

But Kate's eyes were closed in a white, far-away face. Her head was covered in bandages under the bright lights of the hospital room. It all seemed unreal, frightening, and Minty felt angry. Her mother had gone away into a peaceful darkness and left her with strangers. She turned away. 'I want to go,' she said.

'Say a word or two,' said the nurse, kindly.

Minty turned back. 'Hello, Kate . . . Mum . . .' She stopped and looked at the nurse. 'I can't!'

And she ran out of the room, through the hospital and out to the car without stopping.

Later that afternoon, Minty went to see inside Belton House. She walked through the high, quiet rooms and looked at the beautiful furniture. 'Tom won't be here,' she thought. 'The kitchens, that's where he'll be.'

But the kitchens were full of noisy school-children who were looking round the House. Minty turned and went back the way she had come. 'Too crowded,' she thought. She looked out of a window. But the garden was full of visitors, too. 'Later,' she promised herself.

And that evening she went again.

World was in his doorway as she passed. He looked at her kindly. 'That's a worried little face,' he said. 'It's your mother, isn't it? I've been hearing about it, and I'm sorry.' Minty couldn't speak, but World went on quietly, 'You go on to where those children are. You need them now, as much as they need you.'

She walked on through the courtyard to the garden, now empty of visitors. 'It's me, Tom short for Edward!' she said softly. 'I'm here!'

She walked like a sleep-walker towards the sundial. And when she looked up at it, the wind and the voices came again. 'Sundial – moondial!' Her mouth filled with cold air . . . and she felt her hair moving . . . and the ground moving under her . . . Then the wind stopped and the voices were silent. Minty opened her eyes.

Dark! It was night! The moon came from behind a cloud and she saw the House and the smoke from the chimney. It was a night hundreds of years old.

Softly, far away, she heard a child's voice, singing.

'Poor Mary sits a-weeping, a-weeping a-weeping,

'Poor Mary sits a-weeping, on a bright summer's day.'

And then the moon went behind a cloud again.

— 3 —

Children from the past

The child's voice was nearer now.

'Girls and boys come out to play . . .'

And Minty began to sing the same song, her voice shaking.

'The moon is shining bright as day . . .'

'She's younger than me,' thought Minty.

The moon came out from behind the cloud, and there stood a small girl, wearing a cloak. Minty saw part of a small white face before the girl quickly covered it with her hood. 'She's younger than me,' thought Minty.

'Are you from the village?' the girl asked.

'Yes. I'm Araminta Cane,' said Minty. 'Who are you?'

'You haven't heard . . . what they say . . .?'

The girl was frightened, and Minty began to explain that she was not a ghost.

'Sarah! Sarah!' An angry voice came across the garden, and immediately the child ran towards the House.

'I'm sorry! I'm sorry!' she cried.

'There!' came the woman's hard voice. 'Now look what you've done! You've frightened the moon away!'

As she spoke, the moon went behind a cloud and the little girl disappeared. At once Minty felt a new journey in time beginning. She closed her eyes . . . and felt light and darkness, winters and summers flying past her. Then she heard another voice, and knew that she wasn't home yet.

'I've been trying to get you back for days.'

It was Tom. Minty opened her eyes and saw him lying on the ground near the sundial.

'Days?' she said. 'But we only met this morning.'

'It was days ago!' he said.

Minty looked around the garden, and realized that the time of day was different, as well as the year. The first time, she had entered a garden of cool evening shadows, but now she felt the hot sun on her face and arms.

'I know you're a ghost because old Maggs, the gardener, didn't see you the other day,' Tom went on.

'I saw him,' said Minty. 'I touched his coat, and then—' She stopped.

'Then what?'

'He disappeared,' she said slowly. 'And so did you.'

'He didn't disappear for me! I wish he had!'

'Why did you want to see me again?' asked Minty.

'Someone to talk to, I suppose,' he said. 'I get lonely without Dorrie. And you don't run away, like the other one.'

'What – other one?' said Minty.

'My other ghost. She's smaller than you, and she wears long skirts,' he said. 'I always see her at night.'

Minty looked at him. Was it possible that they could both see the same ghost? A ghost from another, and earlier, time? 'What's she like? What's her name?'

'Never seen her face, but her name's Sarah,' he said.

Three people, from three different times, Minty thought. What did it mean? She looked straight at Tom. 'I've seen her too.'

There was a sudden shout. 'Here – you!'

Tom turned quickly and began to run. 'It's Maggs!'

'Wait!' cried Minty. 'I'm coming too!'

He had already disappeared round the corner at the top of the steps, and she almost ran straight into him.

He was standing with his back against a wall, looking into the courtyard. 'I should only go into the garden when I'm sent,' he whispered, 'but I wanted to see you. I'll be in trouble if *she* finds out.'

'She? Who?'

'Mrs Crump,' he said.

Minty looked beyond him, into the courtyard. Now she

19

'I must go!' Tom said. 'Coming?'

knew for sure that it was another century. There was a coach, and men with horses, and footmen giving orders.

'I must go!' Tom said. 'Coming? They won't see you.' And he walked into the courtyard.

Minty followed him to a doorway, and into the House. They went past doors and down stairs, and came to a tunnel, lit by lamps, where the air smelled wet and cold. At the end of the tunnel Minty could smell newly made bread.

'I've got to get in without *her* seeing me!' said Tom.

'So have *I*!' thought Minty.

She heard a voice from the kitchen. 'Clean those pots again, girl.'

Tom went quickly round a half-open door. Minty went after him – and jumped when she heard all the noise. She had never seen so many people in a kitchen!

'Do you hear me, girl?' came the voice again. The speaker was a very large, red-faced woman, and she was hitting a young girl across the head.

'Y–yes, Mrs Crump,' the girl cried.

The kitchen was full of people who seemed to be cleaning pots, or filling them, or banging them. Tom picked up a brush and tried to look busy. Minty felt uncomfortable because people seemed to be looking just past her ear or straight through her. Tom winked at her.

'Here – boy!' Mrs Crump caught hold of Tom's ear.

'Oooowch!' cried Tom.

They came to a tunnel, lit by lamps.

21

'Wink, wink, wink!' With each word, Mrs Crump gave a sharp pull on Tom's ear. 'I won't have winking in my kitchen!' And she pulled him towards the door.

Minty did not want to know if they could walk straight through her. To be invisible was one thing, to be thin air was another. So she jumped quickly out of the way, and into a small dark room near the kitchen door.

Now she was alone, and suddenly loneliness took hold of her. Loneliness and fear, and with them came a picture of her mother's white, still face, and a voice singing in a black night . . .

Poor Mary sits a-weeping, a-weeping, a-weeping . . .

Minty began to weep herself, thinking of her mother, and time moved around her. Then there was warm sunshine on her head and arms . . . She opened her eyes and saw that she was in the garden again, back in her own time.

Next day, Minty went to the hospital without Aunt Mary. Mr Benson came for her after breakfast.

'Feeling better today?' he asked.

'Yes, thanks,' she said, and it was true. It was something to do with yesterday's adventures in the garden, she thought. She could reach Tom and Sarah, who were both lost in time, so perhaps she could reach Kate.

Nothing had changed in the brightly lit hospital room where Kate lay. The nurse gave Minty a chair to sit on.

'Mum, it's me, Minty. Don't go away, please!' said

Minty softly. But nothing moved on that still, white face.

'Where *is* she?' Minty wondered. 'What can I *say* to her?' And at that moment Minty had the idea. She moved nearer to her mother, and began to whisper.

'Mum, I'm going to tell you a story – the story of what's been happening to me. First bit tomorrow, OK?'

She kissed her mother and went to find the doctor, who listened carefully while she explained her idea.

'Wonderful!' he said. 'She can listen to your cassette through headphones. It sounds like a very special story. And she'll hear it, Minty. The one voice in the world that she wants to hear is yours.'

Aunt Mary was in her garden when Minty got back.

'I've had a visitor,' she said. 'Miss Raven.'

Minty felt cold air pass over her body.

'She's writing a book about ghosts,' said Aunt Mary.

'Ghosts?' Minty had a sudden sense of danger. 'Are there any – ghosts?'

'I've never seen any,' said Aunt Mary. 'But Miss Raven wants to investigate. And she's going to stay here, with us! Isn't that exciting?'

The cold air passed over Minty again.

'Someone walking over my grave,' she thought. And then, 'Or theirs.'

Devil's child!

Minty went back to the gardens that afternoon, but there were too many visitors so she walked on to the churchyard. She found herself near the corner of the church, and that same strange icy wind passed over her again. Then she turned, and without surprise saw Tom standing there.

'Cold, isn't it?' he said. 'Like someone walking over my grave.'

'How did it happen this time?' wondered Minty. 'I didn't *feel* anything, so how did I do it?'

'Do what?' Tom said.

'Travel back into your time.'

He smiled. 'You didn't, Miss Clever! I know about the moondial, too. It's *me* who's invisible now!'

'You mean—?' She looked beyond him, into the garden, where the visitors were walking in the afternoon sun. Everything looked very twentieth century.

'Believe me?' he said.

'Yes,' she said, then remembered something. 'Tom, listen! I've got to warn you. Someone is looking for you!'

He laughed. 'No, Maggs and Crump are asleep!'

He looked so happy, but Minty had to warn him. 'Tom, listen! It's a woman from my time—'

'Look at *that*!' he said, not listening to her. 'Ladies with *legs*!' Two women were walking up the path towards them. 'Look at those short skirts! Wait until I tell Dorrie about this!' And he began to dance around the women, making funny faces at them. Minty laughed.

'Hello, dear,' one of the women said to her, unable to see Tom who was making another face behind her.

Minty laughed again – and Tom disappeared.

'Oh!' she cried.

The women moved past her and went into the church.

'Tom! Tom!' whispered Minty. 'Come back!'

But he had gone – back through the time tunnel, and the wind and the voices – back to his own time.

She was standing near a small gravestone which said: *E. L. 1871*. Probably a child's gravestone, she thought. It looked sad, and very – unloved. It made Minty feel sad too, so she went back to the house and began telling her story into her cassette player.

'Dear Mum, this is me, Minty. I'm going to tell you a true story, and only you will hear it . . .' She started with her first meeting with World, and ended with, 'Who is the child

She was standing near a small gravestone.

who hides her face, and who is only seen at night? And who is the strange Miss Raven?'

She turned off the cassette player for a moment, then turned it on again. 'I've been thinking,' she said. 'Moontime – that's where I think *you* are at the moment, so perhaps you'll understand better than me.'

She wondered what happened to time when the moon shone on a sundial. 'I'll go tonight and find out, before that Raven woman gets here,' she decided. 'I want to see the girl in the cloak again, but I mustn't frighten her. I'll try to look like someone from *her* time. I'll wear my long nightdress, and my grey school coat with the hood. It will look like a cloak.'

Then Aunt Mary called and Minty went to help her get Miss Raven's room ready. It was the small room opposite Minty's. 'At least she won't be able to see the church or the house from *her* window,' thought Minty.

'Help me bring in this table, dear,' said Aunt Mary. 'She'll want something to write on. Do you think she'll like that picture? I got it out specially.'

Minty looked at the picture on the wall and her heart jumped. It was an old picture of the moondial! But that was *her* secret. She didn't want Miss Raven sitting and looking at the picture, perhaps realizing that there was some magic about the moondial. Perhaps she would even guess that it was the key which let the children move about in time.

'That picture's a bit – a bit old,' said Minty. 'How about

those photos from my room instead?'

But Aunt Mary wanted the picture to stay and she went on telling Minty about Miss Raven. 'She's a strange woman. She doesn't have a fixed home and just travels around all the time – here, there, and everywhere, she told me.'

Minty did not like the sound of this. A woman who travelled all the time, investigating ghosts. Why? Then she told herself not to be stupid. Miss Raven was probably just a dear old lady who liked ghost stories.

Minty went to bed at nine o'clock. She put on her long nightdress and got into bed. She read her book for a while, then put out the light and listened for the sounds of Aunt Mary going to bed.

At half-past eleven she got up, put on her coat, and softly opened her bedroom door. She listened. The house was silent except for the sound of clocks. She went quietly down the stairs and out into the night.

The moon was large and high in the sky, and seemed to grow brighter as she walked to the churchyard. She pulled up the hood of her coat when she passed by the icy-cold corner of the church.

The tall gates to the garden were shut. Minty tried to open them. 'Locked! Oh, no – no!' She looked around for a way in, then heard a sound.

'Yeeeow!'

Minty turned quickly, just in time to see a cat disappear into the shadows. She followed it between the gravestones and along the side of a high stone wall. She saw another cat in the grass, then another, and *another*. Were they real cats, she wondered, or cats that lived only in moontime?

And then Minty saw a hole in the wall.

It was just big enough for her to climb through, into the garden the other side.

'Now you've done it, Araminta Cane!' she said.

She moved silently towards the moondial as the church clock began to sound midnight. 'I must look at the moondial and see where the shadow falls!' she thought.

With a shock of fear, Minty saw that they had no faces!

But already the jump in time had begun. She could hear the voices and feel the strong wind, as down, down through the dark tunnel of time she went . . .

There was a sudden peace. Minty opened her eyes and found that it was still night. She looked around the moonlit garden.

'Quick! Here!' voices said, but not to her. Minty heard children laughing softly. 'Sssssh!' a voice said.

Minty hid behind a yew tree. Then came the sound of the girl singing.

'Poor Mary sits a-weeping, a-weeping a-weeping,

'Poor Mary sits a-weeping, on a bright summer's day.'

Minty saw the small figure, her face hidden by the hood of her cloak, moving down the steps into the garden. And now Minty saw the others too, moving through the shadows towards the girl. With a shock of fear, Minty saw that they had no faces! Each one wore a sack over its head, with two holes for eyes, and they were coming nearer and nearer.

The girl was at the moondial, looking up. The hood fell back and Minty saw her long straight hair.

'Who *are* you?' she heard the girl say to the statue.

Minty wanted to warn her, but she was afraid of that faceless army with holes for eyes.

'To me you are a moondial!' she heard the girl say.

The faceless army was whispering. 'Moondial . . . moondial . . .' And then the whispers changed to loud calls of 'Devil's child! Devil's child!'

The girl heard them and turned quickly. She gave a little cry and pulled up the hood of her cloak.

'She's got the Eye! The Devil's Eye!'

'No!' cried the girl. 'I haven't! Oh, please!'

'Look at her – hiding it!'

'She's afraid we'll see it! Devil's child! Devil's child!' The faceless army moved nearer and nearer.

'No!' screamed the girl. She pushed herself flat against the statue. 'No!'

'No!' Minty jumped out from behind her tree, ran to the moondial, and put her arms around the little cloaked figure. She felt the girl's heart beating like a frightened animal's, and turned to face the others. 'No!' she said again.

They stopped, and Minty heard them whispering.

'Who is it? A ghost? What?'

Minty saw that they were afraid. She let go of the girl and stepped towards them. 'I am Araminta Cane!' she cried. 'And I have come for you!' Her voice rang across the moonlit garden.

'A ghost!' they cried, and began to scream and run away, some pulling off their sacks, others falling over.

'Whoooo! Wheeee! I'm coming!' cried Minty.

Seconds later the running shadows had disappeared, and the night was silent again. Minty laughed and turned to speak to the frightened girl. But as she turned, a hard angry voice came across the garden.

'Sarah! Sarah! Where are you!' A tall, black figure came down the steps and between the statues.

'Oh, please, please!' cried Sarah.

Minty held out her arms, ready to be a ghost again, but the woman passed her and began to shake the girl angrily.

'Bad, bad child! Back into the house, devil's child!'

'Don't – please don't! I didn't—'

The woman was pulling Sarah back to the house.

'Stop!' cried Minty, but the woman did not see or hear her.

'I have come for you!'

Minty ran and pulled at the woman's cloak . . . but her fingers were empty, and the long black winds of time flew past, taking her back to another night – the night that she had come from.

– 5 –
Miss Vole

Next morning Minty finished the first cassette for her mother, and Mr Benson took it to the hospital. Later on, Miss Raven arrived. She was a tall thin woman with a long white face, and cold eyes. Her clothes were black, and she carried a large black bag. At lunch, Aunt Mary talked to her, but Miss Raven did not listen. She looked at Minty instead.

Then she said, 'What about these ghosts at Belton?'

'I'm afraid I don't know anything about ghosts,' said Aunt Mary.

'And what about you, Araminta?' Miss Raven said softly. 'Perhaps you've seen something?'

'She hasn't been *in* the House yet,' said Aunt Mary. 'Runs around in the garden all day, don't you, Minty?'

'Ah,' said Miss Raven. 'The garden. You must show me the garden, Araminta.'

So after lunch Minty had to take Miss Raven to the garden. As they walked through the yew trees and the statues, Miss Raven looked at Minty, her eyes hard and searching. 'Do you – feel anything?' she asked.

'Feel?' asked Minty. 'I feel a bit hot—'

'I think you know what I mean,' said Miss Raven. 'Have you ever seen a ghost?'

'No!' lied Minty quickly. 'Never!'

'That's strange,' said Miss Raven. 'Because I think you're the kind of child who *could*. *I* have. And my senses tell me that there is something . . . someone . . .' She moved towards the sundial. 'Oh! A sundial!'

'Is it?' Minty said. 'I – I haven't noticed.'

'How interesting!' Miss Raven looked carefully at the sundial, then said, 'Come! Let's move on.'

She looked around and noticed the church.

'I must see that,' she said. And as they went through the tall gates, a black cat appeared between the gravestones.

'Oh! A sundial!'

'How beautiful!' she said. 'Cat! Cat!'

The cat looked at Miss Raven and walked over to her. She picked it up in her arms and held it lovingly.

Minty watched, wondering. Then, 'Witches have cats!' she thought.

During tea that afternoon Minty ate silently, thinking about her ghosts. She had met Tom and Sarah, in their different times, and Tom and Sarah had also met each other. It was like a dance in time, but what did it all mean? She felt that it was important for all three of them to meet together – and she felt that it would happen soon.

After tea Miss Raven brought out the photographs to show them. 'I am very interested in photographs,' she said. 'When the camera *CLICKS!*, that moment of time is trapped forever! It's why I'm also interested in ghosts, who are already trapped, of course – trapped in their past.'

Minty, watching her, thought, 'She wants to make Tom and Sarah prisoners – to trap them in time. But I'll stop her. That's why I'm here.'

Minty woke at five o'clock the next morning. She opened her door quietly, not wanting to wake the witch Raven from her dark dreams, and went quickly out of the house.

She climbed through the hole in the churchyard wall again, and began to run – because she was cold, but also because she was excited. At the moondial she spoke to the statue of the boy.

She was moving towards a garden pool.

'It's me again,' she told him. 'Araminta Cane.'

She touched his cold stone head, and immediately time moved around her and she came into a different morning. Where was Tom? Was this his time? Sarah belonged to the night.

'Minty!' He was behind one of the yew trees. 'Quick! Here!' he whispered.

Minty obeyed. 'What's wrong? Maggs about?'

'No! Not *born* yet, probably!'

'*What?*' said Minty.

'Shhh! Listen!' he said.

And then she heard the voice singing.

'Poor Mary sits-a-weeping, a-weeping, a-weeping.'

'She's here!' whispered Minty. 'In *your* time!'

'No! We're *there*!' he said. 'In *her* time. Come on – we can meet her, talk to her.'

Sarah had her back to them. She was wearing a soft blue cloak with the hood down, and was moving towards the edge of a large garden pool behind some trees.

'No, I mustn't look,' they heard her say. 'But if I wash my face in the water, will that make it go?' She washed her face, then looked up at the sky. 'There. Let the sun dry it. Oh, *please* make it go, please!'

Minty guessed that Sarah's eyes were shut as she waited for the sun to dry her face. At last, Sarah shook her head and slowly put a hand up to her face.

'*Feels* the same . . .' they heard her say. 'But how can I know? But I mustn't look at my face in the pool, I mustn't!'

Tom could wait no longer. 'Sarah!' he said.

The child turned quickly. Her hand flew up to her face again. But not before Minty saw the dark purple birthmark on one side of it. *Now* she understood.

'Oh Sarah!' she whispered, and moved quickly towards her.

But the girl was running away like a frightened animal. 'Sarah! Stop! Please!'

'After her!' shouted Tom.

Minty saw the girl's head turn, and saw her frightened face. 'No, Tom!' Minty said. 'She thinks we're like those other children! Did you – see her face?'

'Yes,' said Tom. 'Poor little devil.'

'Don't say that! Not – devil! It's what *they* said.'

They saw her disappear behind the large yew trees at the end of the path to the house. Then they followed, and saw her enter the house through the door that Minty had used with Tom.

They ran inside and saw her pass through a door. They reached it just in time to see her go through another door on the far side of the room. It was a room with big heavy furniture, and large pictures on the walls. Tom looked around in fear.

'Wait!' he cried. 'This is the Breakfast Room. They'll beat me for a week if they catch me in here!'

'They can't see you! It's *her* time, remember?'

They went through the second door now, and into a room where the carpet, walls, and furniture were all red.

'The Red Room!' said Tom. 'I've never been in here, but I've heard about it. Strange, isn't it?'

Minty went through it to a large entrance hall where Sarah's small blue figure was already halfway across. A young woman carrying a brush came round a corner. She saw Sarah's purple face, and screamed.

'Oh! No! Save me! Save me from the evil eye!' she cried,

Sarah's small blue figure was already halfway across.

and covered her eyes. She ran past Sarah – and past Minty and Tom, without seeing them.

'We *are* invisible!' said Tom.

Sarah turned slowly. She was crying. 'It's still there!' she said. Then she saw Tom and Minty, but did not seem to care. 'Who are you?'

'We want to help you,' said Minty. 'We're friends.'

'Aren't you – afraid of me?' said Sarah. 'The others are. They call me devil's—'

'I know what they call you,' Minty said quickly. 'But you're not!'

Another voice made all three of them jump. '*Sarah*!'

Sarah turned and ran. 'I'm coming, Miss Vole! I'm coming!'

'Little devil! What have I told you?'

Sarah disappeared round a corner. Then Minty and Tom heard Miss Vole hitting her, and they went after her.

Miss Vole was pulling Sarah up the stairs.

'Stop! Stop!' screamed Minty, and ran after them. She got to the first turn in the stairs and saw them in a doorway above her. Then the door was banged shut.

Tom and Minty reached the top of the stairs together.

'We're going in!' said Minty.

Tom was shocked and afraid. He was only a kitchen boy and these rooms were like another world to him.

'We have to help her,' whispered Minty.

'All right,' whispered Tom, but he was shaking with fear.

Minty opened the door silently and they went inside. Miss Vole was speaking to Sarah, very softly.

'Do you know what it's like for me, shut up here, week after week, with a devil's child?'

They were in a bedroom where everything was yellow and there were long curtains all round the walls. Miss Vole's tall black back stood between them and the windows, and Sarah's small figure was hidden behind her.

'They don't pay me very much,' the soft, frightening voice continued. 'No one speaks to me. Do you know why, Sarah? Because they're afraid of me. They believe some of the evil must pass from you to me because I'm with you every day. And perhaps they're right.'

Sarah did not reply, but Minty could hear her crying.

'I sometimes wonder if I'm here . . . If I'm real . . .' the voice continued. 'Perhaps I shall go crazy . . .'

There was a silence.

Then Miss Vole said, 'Why don't you look at me? *Look* at me!'

She moved quickly past Sarah and pulled back one of the yellow curtains. Behind it was a long mirror.

Sarah screamed and covered her face with her hands.

Minty almost screamed, too – *because the face that she saw in the mirror was the face of Miss Raven*!

'I'm still here,' said Miss Vole. 'The mirror tells me I am. Do you think I'm beautiful, Sarah? Do you?' Miss Vole turned quickly and shook her. 'Answer me!'

'Oh yes – yes!'

'The mirrors are coming out to play.'

'And beautiful faces need mirrors! Better hide your head, dear. The mirrors are coming out to play!'

And she began to pull back the yellow curtains from the mirrors that were all round the room. Sarah ran and jumped on to the bed and pulled her hood over her face.

'How different the room looks now!' said Miss Vole. 'I wish you could see it. But you can't, can you? We know what will happen if *you* ever look in a mirror, don't we,

40

Sarah? What will happen? Tell me!'

'The – glass will – break,' whispered Sarah.

Miss Vole laughed. 'Yes! And then . . .?'

'Oh no, please!' cried Sarah. 'The – the devil—'

'The devil will get you!' said that terrible voice.

Tom could not listen any more. He pulled open the bedroom door and ran down the stairs.

Miss Vole looked at the open door. 'Who is it?'

'Her turn to be afraid,' thought Minty. She ran after Tom and found him in the Red Room. He was holding on to a chair and coughing painfully, his thin body shaking as he coughed.

'Why did you run?' Minty said. 'We ought to help her.'

The hard, dry cough was terrible to hear, and he could not speak at first. At last he managed to say, 'You heard what she said. The devil!'

Minty looked at him. Surely he didn't believe that little Sarah was the devil's child! And then she saw the blood at the corner of his mouth.

'Oh Tom!' she whispered.

'I'm finished!' he said. 'With her – and you! No more devil's games for me. I'm going to grow tall and be a footman, I'm going to bring Dorrie here and—'

His thin shape was disappearing as he spoke . . . and then he was gone. He had left her alone. Minty knew that it was useless to call him back. He had gone because he wanted to go.

She went back through the rooms and into the

41

courtyard. There were people and horses there but they did not see her. In her head Miss Vole's voice was saying, '*Better hide your head, dear. The mirrors are coming out to play! . . . The devil will get you!*'

Minty ran back to the moondial.

'I want to go home!' she cried. 'I want to go home!'

– 6 –
'Someone walking over my grave . . .'

'So *there* you are!' said Aunt Mary.

'Am I late?' said Minty. 'Sorry.'

'I wondered where you were,' said Aunt Mary. She and Miss Raven had already started breakfast.

'Perhaps you've been out all night,' said Miss Raven. Then after a moment added, 'Have you?'

'No!' said Minty. 'I just got up early.'

She escaped to her room after breakfast to tell her most recent adventure to the cassette for her mother.

When she came down, Miss Raven had gone to the House – to investigate, Aunt Mary said. Minty went to see World, and found him sitting in the doorway of his lodge.

'How's your mother?' he asked her.

'Oh, she's getting better, thank you,' said Minty. 'But . . . but invisibly.' She went on quickly, 'I wanted to ask you, do you know anything about that moon – sundial?

42

The one with the man and the boy.'

'Chronos and Eros,' said World. 'That's their Greek names. Chronos is Time.'

'Time!' said Minty, suddenly excited.

'Yes. And Eros – the small boy with the wings – he's Love.'

'Of course!' said Minty.

And Love will win its fight with Time in the battle to make Tom and Sarah free, she thought.

World looked at her. 'Those children . . .' he said quietly. 'They're in trouble. I can still hear them crying.'

'I know,' Minty said. 'But not for much longer, I promise.'

'Mr Benson phoned,' Aunt Mary told her when she got back. 'He says he'll come for you at two o'clock.'

Later, when Minty heard Mr Benson's car, she pushed the cassette into her pocket and ran outside.

'Is Mum . . .?' began Minty.

'Do you want me to tell you, or do you want to wait and see?' he said.

'Oh, wait and see, I suppose! But hurry!'

Her mother was still asleep in the hospital bed. On the table, Minty saw her cassette player with the first cassette in it, and the headphones next to it.

'Say hello to her,' said the nurse. 'I'll be back in a minute,' and she left the two of them together.

Minty touched her mother's arm. 'Mum, it's me, Minty,'

she said. 'Did you listen to my story? There's lots more to tell you. I went again, and—'

She stopped. Her mother's eyes were opening. She was looking straight into Minty's own eyes.

'Minty . . .' she whispered. 'Minty!'

'Oh Mum . . . Mum . . . you've come back!' cried Minty.

'Oh Mum . . . Mum . . . you've come back!'

'*Was* it my story that brought her back?' asked Minty, when she and Mr Benson were driving back to Belton. Kate had not spoken again during the visit, but she was on the way back to the real world and would come a little more each day, the doctor had said.

'I'm sure it was,' said Mr Benson.

Aunt Mary was pleased, too. 'Well, that *is* lovely news,' she said. 'Did she have much to say?'

'No, just my name,' said Minty.

'There's a long way to go yet then,' said Miss Raven, looking at them with cold eyes. Then she said to Aunt Mary, 'There's an interesting sundial in the House gardens, with two stone figures. Eros and Chronos, I'm told.'

'*She* knows their names, too!' thought Minty.

She went out, not because she had anywhere to go, but to escape from her aunt and Miss Raven.

'I'll go to the churchyard,' she thought. 'I'll sit in that cold place. It must mean something, and perhaps I'll find out what it is if I sit and wait.'

She sat on the grass, looking up at the top of the church, and the wind was cold on her face and arms. Then she began to feel another kind of cold.

'Someone walking over my grave,' she thought, 'or – something!'

'Minty! Minty!' came a whisper.

Tom was standing a few metres away, just inside the high gates, and his face was white and afraid.

'Tom!' she cried. She jumped up and went to him, and

45

he looked at her without speaking. 'Come on, Tom. Over here.' She took him to the far side of the churchyard, and he lay down and began to cry. 'What is it, Tom? Tell me, please.'

After a long time, he said, 'Dorrie . . . my sister . . . she's coughing blood!'

'Oh – Tom!' Minty could find no other words to say.

He pushed a hand across his eyes. 'Crying won't help,' he said. 'Dorrie doesn't cry. Do you know what she does? Screams! You should hear her!'

'I feel like screaming, too,' said Minty. She felt angry inside. What terrible lives children like Tom and Dorrie had! Ill, no friends or family to care for them, and never a kind word from anyone.

Tom looked at her. 'We've got to get Sarah out, haven't we?' he said.

'Yes,' agreed Minty. 'And we've got to get *you* out.'

'Me? How will *I* get out? And where?'

'Into moontime,' said Minty. 'But I don't know how yet.'

They were all in this game together – Kate, herself, Tom, Sarah. She looked at Tom. He was her friend but he was also a kitchen boy from a hundred years ago, here with her *now*. He was not a ghost, he was real – a boy with a dirty face and untidy hair. And she knew that if this moment was real, all things were possible.

'We're *all* real!' she laughed.

He jumped up from the grass. 'And I'll grow tall and be

a footman or my name's not Teddy Larkin!'

'What did you say your name was?' she said.

'Teddy Larkin, of course.'

'But – you said it was Tom! Tom short for Edward!'

'It's Teddy, short for Edward,' he said, 'but kitchen boys here are always called Tom.'

'*All* kitchen boys?' she said.

'That's right. There's three of us, all Toms.'

Then he started coughing. It was painful to hear.

'Tom!' Minty said. 'We'll meet by the moondial. Midnight, tonight. Will you do it?'

'I'll try,' he said, when he could speak again. 'I came to tell you about Dorrie. I – had to tell you.'

'You needed me, and I needed you when we first met.'

'And Sarah – she needs us both,' said Tom.

It was as easy as that, Minty thought. Nothing difficult about moontime. It was the most natural thing in the world.

— 7 —

The end of the game

'Miss Raven is going to the House to look for ghosts tonight, Minty,' said Aunt Mary that evening.

'Make sure you don't look in a mirror!' Minty was shocked to hear her own voice say the words.

'What?' Miss Raven's voice was sharp.

'It's – just something I heard,' said Minty. 'If you see a ghost in a mirror – the devil gets you!'

'Minty!' She heard her aunt's shocked voice.

'I – I've never heard anything so stupid!' said Miss Raven. She turned quickly and went out of the room.

At half-past eleven that night, Minty looked out of her bedroom window and saw Miss Raven going down the path wearing a long black cloak with a hood. Minty waited until she had gone, then went softly out of her room, down the stairs and out of the house.

Tom was waiting for her in the garden, beside the moondial. They looked at the statue of the man and the boy, white in the moonlight.

'It's the boy that will help us,' said Minty. And she put

Very slowly, he put his hand next to hers.

her hand on the boy's head. 'Now you, Tom!'

Very slowly, he put his hand next to hers.

The next moment their ears were filled with whispers and voices, and the wind blew clean and cold as they went back . . . back in time . . .

When the wind and the voices stopped, Minty knew that they were under a different moon at a different time of year. The air was sharp and cold, and the moon shone over trees that had lost most of their leaves.

'Look!' whispered Tom.

And she saw the small cloaked figure coming down the steps and into the garden. 'Sarah!'

'Where's she going?' said Tom.

They watched her walk between the yew trees and across the grass, away from them.

'She's going to the pool!' said Minty.

They followed, staying in the shadows until they saw her by the round pool, silver in the moonlight.

'One more try,' they heard her say. 'The magic night of all the year . . . Hallowe'en!'

Hallowe'en! The word filled Minty with fear and excitement. Hallowe'en, when all the ghosts in the world went free! Tom was holding her arm and she knew that he, who half-believed in the devil, was a thousand times more frightened than she was.

Sarah began to wash her face in the pool. Minty and Tom were watching her and did not notice the strange shapes coming out of the shadows of the trees.

Sarah lifted her face up to the moon.

And then Minty and Tom saw the shapes move round her in a half-circle. They wore cloaks, and frightening masks with holes for eyes. They carried lamps made from pumpkins, like lighted heads without bodies.

Then the whispering began:

'Devil's child, devil's child, devil's child!'

Sarah looked round wildly and screamed. She ran straight through the circle, and Tom and Minty went with her. The circle broke with screams and shouts.

'After her! Get her!'

Sarah ran to a stone wall and fell against it as Tom and Minty reached her. 'No! Oh no!' she cried.

'Sarah! We're here!' Minty held her, but Sarah pulled her hand away and put it up to her face.

The children with their Hallowe'en masks were only a

metre or two away now. Minty turned to them.

'Do you know who I am?' Her voice was a whisper. 'We have met before! I am Araminta Cane, and I am a ghost!'

One small figure ran from the crowd, dropping his lamp as he went. 'I'm going!' he said.

The others did not move.

'She's not a ghost,' said one voice.

'Who's that other one?' said another.

'Do as I say,' Minty went on, 'and you will not be hurt! Soon it will be midnight – midnight on Hallowe'en! The magic hour! Go back to the pool and drop your lamps into the water. When the clock begins to sound the twelve hours of midnight, shut your eyes. If you open them before the clock finishes, then . . .' She stopped.

'The *devil* will get you!' Tom said suddenly.

'Devil's child, devil's child, devil's child!'

51

They ran, screaming, down to the pool and dropped their lamps into the water. As the last light died, the clock on the House began to sound the hours.

The children stood unmoving by the pool, and Minty knew that their eyes were shut against the coming of the devil.

'Quick! Now!' she said to Tom and Sarah.

Hand in hand, the three of them ran across the moonlit grass and hid in the trees . . . ten . . . eleven . . . twelve! Then the clock was silent. A second later came a shout.

'They've gone! Find them!'

And the search began. Dark shapes moved among the trees, and Minty saw a masked face only a metre away.

Then a voice whispered, 'Sam! I'm going!'

'And me! Before the devil gets us, too!'

Feet began to run, and voices shouted.

'Come on! Run!'

'The devil's after us!'

And then there was silence.

'They've gone,' said Tom.

Minty took Sarah over to the moondial, and Tom followed. 'Sarah,' Minty said softly. 'You can put your hood down now. It's safe. Please, Sarah. *Please*!'

Slowly, very slowly, a hand came up and pulled the hood away. Sarah, her purple birthmark clear in the moonlight, looked first at Minty and then at Tom.

Minty moved towards her – and kissed the birthmark. Sarah looked at her, unable to believe it. Then Minty took

'That's – me?'

something from her pocket. It shone in the moonlight, and
Sarah's hands flew up to cover her eyes.

'*A mirror!*' she cried.

'Open your eyes,' said Minty. 'Don't be afraid.'

After a moment, Sarah let her hands fall.

'I'm holding the mirror,' said Minty, 'and I want you to
look in it. Don't be afraid.'

Tom took Sarah's hand and held it. 'Go on!' he said.

Sarah looked, and her hand touched the mirror, very
gently. 'That's – me?' she said. 'I'm – beautiful!'

'Oh, you are, you are!' said Minty.

'And the mirror didn't break!' said Sarah.

'Of course it didn't!' said Tom.

Another voice came across the garden – sharp and cold. 'Sarah! Sarah!' And the tall black figure of a woman came towards them.

'Oh, I must go!' cried Sarah.

But Tom pulled her against him and held her. 'Come with me, Sarah!' He kissed her face. 'I've come a long way to fetch you. Come with me!'

The woman came quickly. 'Devil's child! Come here!'

Minty stepped in front of Sarah and Tom and held up the mirror to that wild white face. 'The devil's here!' she cried. 'Take care!' There was a scream, the sharp sound of breaking glass – and then a silence.

Afterwards, what happened next seemed like a dream to Minty. She remembered a black circle on the ground, like a dead fire, where the woman had stood, and a great wind blowing through the garden. At the far end of the path, a white bird flew into the air. Minty watched it until someone called her name, and then she saw Tom and Sarah, hand in hand, running away, their feet in a kind of cloud. They smiled at her and for a moment she wanted to go after them, to run free for ever in moontime, in a world that never changed. But the moondial was pulling her back . . . back . . .

And she thought afterwards that she remembered another child running in the cloud. A little figure calling,

Minty held up the mirror to that wild white face.

'Teddy! Teddy!' Then Tom shouting, 'Dorrie!' Then the three figures met and ran on . . . and on, until they disappeared.

Minty did not remember touching the moondial, or the last long jump forward in time, or the winds and the lost voices in the tunnel.

But she knew that the strange game was over.

*   *   *

Next morning she found the broken mirror in the pocket of her grey coat. And when she went downstairs for breakfast, Miss Raven had gone.

'Did she disappear into thin air?' asked Minty.

'Of course not, dear. She took Mr Jones's taxi to the station,' said Aunt Mary.

The telephone rang and she went to answer it.

'It's the hospital!' she called to Minty after a moment. 'It's your mother – she's asking for you! Mr Benson will be here in an hour to take you to her.'

During that hour Minty went to tell World what had happened, but she saw at once that he already knew.

'I was right,' he said. 'You *were* the one.'

'Yes,' said Minty. 'They're free. And my mother is awake – she's asking for me!'

He laughed. 'I'm so pleased. So the work is done.'

'Yes.' Each seemed to know what the other meant. There was no need to put it into words.

She walked on to the garden, but it was calm and quiet now. The moondial looked the same – two winged figures locked together in a battle that would never end. Minty touched the cold head of the boy, but nothing happened.

Then she went on to the churchyard, to the corner of the church – and the icy wind was still there.

'It's a mystery!' she said.

And then she saw the small gravestone: *E. L. 1871.*

She thought of Tom. He seemed so real, so near.

'Of course! Teddy . . . Edward! E. L. – Edward Larkin!'

And she remembered that day when he had suddenly appeared here, on this corner, saying, 'Somebody walking over my grave!'

She thought of Tom and Sarah, hand in hand, running off into moontime, to meet Dorrie, and she knew that the circle of time was complete.

GLOSSARY

birthmark a red or purple mark on a person's skin from birth

coma a very deep sleep, usually because a person's head has been badly hurt

cough *(v)* to send out air from the throat in a noisy way

devil the strongest and worst of all evil ghosts

evil very bad

footman a man who works in the house of an important or rich family, opening doors to visitors, etc.

Hallowe'en 31st October, when people say that the ghosts of dead people come back to the living world

investigate to discover and study all the facts about something

invisible (something/somebody) that you cannot see

kiss *(v)* to touch someone with the lips in a loving way

lodge a small house at the entrance to the gardens of a large house

magic something which makes impossible things happen

purple a red-blue colour

shock *(n)* a sudden and very unpleasant surprise

sixth sense being able to know something although you can't see, hear, touch, taste, or smell it

sundial a flat piece of metal, marked with the hours, which uses shadows made by the sun to show the time

trapped unable to escape

tunnel a long hole under the ground

weeping crying

wink to close and open one eye, as a secret message to someone

witch a woman who uses magic to do things (usually, but not always, bad things)

Moondial

ACTIVITIES

Before Reading

1 Read the story introduction on the first page of the book, and the back cover. What do you know now about the story? Find answers to these questions.

1 How is Minty Cane different from other people?
2 Where is the moondial?
3 Why is it called a moondial, not a sundial?
4 How does Minty travel into the past?
5 How far back in time does Minty travel?
6 Which three people does she meet in the past?

2 What do you think is going to happen in this story? Choose Y (Yes) or N (No) for each of these ideas.

1 Minty is the only person to discover the secret of the moondial. Y/N
2 Minty travels into the future as well as the past. Y/N
3 Tom travels from his own time into Minty's time. Y/N
4 Sarah also travels into Minty's time. Y/N
5 Sarah becomes Minty's best friend. Y/N
6 Minty is able to help both Tom and Sarah. Y/N
7 Minty brings Sarah and Tom together, across the years. Y/N
8 Miss Vole stops Minty returning to her own time. Y/N
9 Minty destroys the 'evil Miss Vole'. Y/N

While Reading

Read page 1, and Chapters 1 and 2. Choose the best question-word for these questions, and then answer them.

What / Who / Why

1 . . . does the person in the garden on page 1 hear?
2 . . . can the person in the garden see at their feet?
3 . . . did Minty think she was a witch, or something like it?
4 . . . did Minty go to stay with?
5 . . . felt cold in the churchyard?
6 . . . happened to Minty's mother on her way home?
7 . . . did World seem pleased that Minty had come?
8 . . . did Minty want Tom to shake hands with her?
9 . . . did Minty learn about Tom's family?
10 . . . couldn't Kate talk to Minty after the car crash?

Before you read Chapters 3 and 4 (*Children from the past* and *Devil's child!*), can you guess what happens next? Choose endings for these sentences.

1 The child who is singing is . . .
   a) a girl called Sarah.   b) Tom.   c) Tom's sister, Dorrie.
2 The 'Devil's child' will be . . .
   a) Minty herself.   b) Tom.   c) Sarah.
3 Minty begins to tell the story of her time travels to . . .
   a) Aunt Mary.   b) her mother.   c) Mr Benson.

Read Chapters 3 and 4. Who said this, and to whom? What, or who, were they talking about?

1 'Days? But we only met this morning.'
2 'She's smaller than you, and she wears long skirts.'
3 'I won't have winking in my kitchen!'
4 'She can listen to your cassette through headphones.'
5 'I've never seen any. But Miss Raven wants to investigate.'
6 'Cold, isn't it? Like someone walking over my grave.'
7 'Moontime – that's where I think *you* are at the moment.'
8 'She doesn't have a fixed home, and just travels around all the time – here, there, and everywhere.'
9 'She's got the Eye! The Devil's Eye!'
10 'I am Araminta Cane! And I have come for you!'

Before you read Chapters 5 and 6 (*Miss Vole* and '*Someone walking over my grave . . .*'), what do you think is going to happen? Choose Y (Yes) or N (No) for each of these ideas.

1 Miss Raven discovers the secret of the moondial. Y/N
2 Minty has a strong feeling that Miss Raven is a witch. Y/N
3 Minty discovers why people call Sarah 'devil's child'. Y/N
4 Minty helps Miss Raven investigate the ghosts. Y/N
5 Minty, Tom, and Sarah meet and talk to each other. Y/N

Read Chapters 5 and 6. Here are some untrue sentences. Rewrite them with the correct information.

1 Minty wanted to help Miss Raven find some ghosts.
2 Tom and Minty travelled to a future time, to meet Sarah.

3 Sarah was miserable because she had no friends.

4 Miss Vole was very kind to Sarah in the room of mirrors.

5 Sarah believed that the glass would break if she looked through a window.

6 Tom showed no fear of Miss Vole or of the devil.

7 The names of the sundial statues were Death and the Devil.

8 Listening to Minty's story was making it difficult for Kate to return to the real world.

9 Tom came to tell Minty that his sister Dorrie was dead.

10 Minty wanted to bring Tom and Sarah out of their sad lives into her own time.

11 Minty realized that Tom and Sarah were only ghosts, not real people.

12 Kitchen boys at Belton House were always called Teddy.

Before you read Chapter 7 (*The end of the game*), can you guess how the story ends? Choose some of these ideas.

1 Tom and Minty meet and travel back to Sarah's time.

2 They find Sarah weeping in the room of mirrors.

3 The village children throw stones at Sarah in the garden.

4 Minty makes Sarah look in a mirror.

5 Minty makes Miss Vole look in a mirror.

6 The mirror doesn't break for either of them.

7 Tom, Sarah, and Dorrie escape into moontime.

8 The gravestone which says *E. L. 1871* has disappeared the next time Minty goes to the churchyard.

9 Minty's mother dies in hospital.

After Reading

1 **Perhaps this is what some of the characters in the story were thinking. Which characters are they, and what is happening in the story at this moment?**

1 'Yes, she's the one, all right. I can always tell. She knew what I was talking about at once. She doesn't understand everything yet, but she knows she's here for a reason, and she knows she'll find out what it is soon . . .'

2 'How beautiful the pool is in the moonlight! Surely if I wash my face in it tonight, the most magic night of the year . . . Oh, the water's cold! Please, please make it go . . .'

3 'I can't believe it! Why *do* people drive so fast these days! In a coma – how awful! Who knows if she'll ever . . . And that poor little girl! How am I going to break it to her? Only just arrived, and this has to happen!'

4 'This child knows more about the Belton ghosts than she's telling. I feel sure she's seen them. I must keep a close eye on her. I'll get her to show me the garden, for a start . . .'

5 'Ooh, my ear really hurts! Why did old Crump have to pull it so hard? All I did was wink at my ghost – oh, where is she? She's gone, disappeared. Hope she'll be back soon. She's more fun to talk to than the kitchen boys here . . .'

2 Perhaps Tom was able to get down to London to see Dorrie when he heard she was ill (see page 46). Here is their conversation. Put it in the right order, and write in the speaker's names. Tom speaks first (number 5).

1 _____ 'No, not yet. Footmen have to be tall, so I've got to grow a bit first. But listen, Dorrie. I've met a ghost!'

2 _____ 'Trousers! Girls don't wear trousers, Teddy!'

3 _____ 'You needn't laugh, Dorrie – it's all true. Ooh, I don't like the sound of that cough of yours . . .'

4 _____ 'In the kitchen? You're not a footman yet, then?'

5 _____ 'Hullo, Dorrie. How are you?'

6 _____ 'Oh, you can travel into the future as well, can you? My word, you'll be head footman any day now!'

7 _____ 'I'm doing fine. But it's hard work in the kitchen, and they don't seem to like boys from London much.'

8 _____ 'You've met what? Oh, Teddy, you were dreaming!'

9 _____ 'Well, this one does, Miss Clever! And ladies in her time wear short skirts. You can see their legs!'

10 _____ 'Not very well, Teddy. I can't stop coughing, you see. But never mind that. How are you getting on?'

11 _____ 'No, I wasn't, Dorrie! I promise. Her name's Minty. She's from the future – and she wears trousers!'

3 What are these three things usually used for, and what special uses did they have in the story?

1 a sundial
2 a cassette player
3 a mirror

4 There are 23 words (4 letters or longer) from the story in this word search. Find the words (they go from left to right, and from top to bottom), and draw lines through them.

C	I	S	U	N	D	I	A	L	W	C	O	M	A
H	A	N	I	N	V	I	S	I	B	L	E	T	Y
U	C	O	U	T	W	I	N	K	C	O	U	G	H
R	A	O	L	G	I	O	O	G	P	A	T	H	K
C	S	B	I	R	T	H	M	A	R	K	I	O	S
H	S	N	I	A	C	O	A	R	T	P	A	S	T
Y	E	D	O	V	H	O	G	D	N	O	T	T	A
A	T	W	E	E	P	D	I	E	B	O	E	A	T
R	T	F	E	V	I	L	C	N	R	L	A	I	U
D	E	V	I	L	C	E	N	T	U	R	Y	D	E

5 Here is a piece from Minty's cassette for her mother. Use 12 of the words from the word search to complete the passage.

'I went back to the ＿＿＿＿ this morning, and when I touched the ＿＿＿＿ of the boy, it took me straight back into the ＿＿＿＿. Tom was waiting for me, and we saw Sarah washing her face in the ＿＿＿＿. Oh, Mum, it's so sad! Now I know why she hides her face behind the ＿＿＿＿ of her ＿＿＿＿. She's got a ＿＿＿＿ on her face, and that's why they call her ＿＿＿＿'s child and say she has the ＿＿＿＿ eye. And poor Tom has this terrible ＿＿＿＿. I must help them both, but how? And there's this woman, Miss Raven, staying with Aunt Mary. A black cat came up to her in the ＿＿＿＿ – I'm sure she's a ＿＿＿＿ . . .'

6 **Look at the word search again, and write down all the letters that don't have a line through them. Begin with the first line, and go across each line to the end. You should have 30 letters, which will make 10 words, in 2 sentences.**

    1 What are the two sentences? Who said them, to whom?

    2 What was the 'it', and how did the listener feel about it?

    3 Did this thing help anybody? If so, how?

    4 What happened to this thing in the end?

7 **Would you like to travel in time, like Minty? Which of these possibilities would you choose, and why?**

I would like to travel . . .

- five / a hundred / a thousand / ten thousand years
- into the future / the past
- in my own country / a foreign country.

I would like to meet . . .

- famous people / ordinary people / people from my own family.

I would never choose to travel in time, even if it was possible.

8 **Do you agree (A) or disagree (D) with these ideas? Why?**

    1 There are no ghosts. People only *think* they see them.

    2 Everything that happens can be explained, using scientific facts. No sensible person believes in magic or witches.

    3 Some people *do* have a sixth sense, which cannot be explained by science.

ABOUT THE AUTHOR

Helen Cresswell was born in Nottingham, in central England, in 1934, and started writing stories at the age of seven. She studied at London University, and was a teacher before becoming a full-time writer of children's books. Her early books were of two kinds: stories about magical worlds, like *Where the Wind Blows*, or funny stories about real life, like *Jumbo Spencer*. Her first widely successful book, *The Piemakers*, combined both types of writing, and was soon followed by *The Night-Watchmen*, which won her the Phoenix Award. She went on to write many more books in the late 1960s and early 70s. Then in 1973, when she was asked to write for the BBC children's television programme *Jackanory*, she wrote the very popular *Lizzie Dripping* stories. She has adapted or written many more stories for television since then.

In *Moondial* (1987), she returns to the world of magic, witches, and evil. The idea for the story came from Belton House, a National Trust house and garden in Lincolnshire, which can be visited by the public. A television adaptation of *Moondial* was filmed there in 1988. In the book the garden is described just as it is in real life, with its paths and yew trees, and the sundial statue of Chronos and Eros.

Helen Cresswell has written over a hundred books for children and is also well known for her television writing, especially *Lizzie Dripping*, *The Bagthorpe Saga*, *The Secret World of Polly Flint*, and *Moondial*. She still lives in Nottinghamshire, a stone's throw from Robin Hood's Sherwood Forest.

ABOUT BOOKWORMS

OXFORD BOOKWORMS LIBRARY
Classics • True Stories • Fantasy & Horror • Human Interest
Crime & Mystery • Thriller & Adventure

The OXFORD BOOKWORMS LIBRARY offers a wide range of original and adapted stories, both classic and modern, which take learners from elementary to advanced level through six carefully graded language stages:

Stage 1 (400 headwords)	**Stage 4** (1400 headwords)
Stage 2 (700 headwords)	**Stage 5** (1800 headwords)
Stage 3 (1000 headwords)	**Stage 6** (2500 headwords)

More than fifty titles are also available on cassette, and there are many titles at Stages 1 to 4 which are specially recommended for younger learners. In addition to the introductions and activities in each Bookworm, resource material includes photocopiable test worksheets and Teacher's Handbooks, which contain advice on running a class library and using cassettes, and the answers for the activities in the books.

Several other series are linked to the OXFORD BOOKWORMS LIBRARY. They range from highly illustrated readers for young learners, to playscripts, non-fiction readers, and unsimplified texts for advanced learners.

Oxford Bookworms Starters	*Oxford Bookworms Factfiles*
Oxford Bookworms Playscripts	*Oxford Bookworms Collection*

Details of these series and a full list of all titles in the OXFORD BOOKWORMS LIBRARY can be found in the *Oxford English* catalogues. A selection of titles from the OXFORD BOOKWORMS LIBRARY can be found on the next pages.

BOOKWORMS • HUMAN INTEREST • STAGE 3

The Secret Garden

FRANCES HODGSON BURNETT

Retold by Clare West

Little Mary Lennox is a bad-tempered, disagreeable child. When her parents die in India, she is sent back to England to live with her uncle in a big, lonely, old house.

There is nothing to do all day except walk in the gardens – and watch the robin flying over the high walls of the secret garden . . . which has been locked for ten years. And no one has the key.

BOOKWORMS • FANTASY & HORROR • STAGE 3

The Star Zoo

HARRY GILBERT

In our world today a hummingbird is a small, brilliantly coloured bird that lives in the tall trees of tropical forests.

In the far distant future, Hummingbird (Hummy for short) is a girl of sixteen who lives somewhere in the Galaxy, on a planet called Just Like Home. She has the name 'Hummingbird' in big letters on all her clothes, but she has never seen a real hummingbird. She has never seen any living animal or bird at all. The Book of Remembering says that there were once many animals on a planet called Earth, but that was before the Burning, a long, long time ago . . .

On the Edge

GILLIAN CROSS

Retold by Clare West

When Tug wakes up, he is not in his own bedroom at home. The door is locked and there are bars across the window. Loud music hammers through the house and through his head. Then a woman comes in and says that she is his mother, but Tug knows that she is *not* his mother . . .

Outside, Jinny stares through the trees at the lonely house on the hill. She hears strange noises, but she turns away. After all, it's none of her business . . .

The Crown of Violet

GEOFFREY TREASE

Retold by John Escott

High up on a stone seat in the great open-air theatre of Athens, Alexis, son of Leon, watches the Festival of Plays – and dreams of seeing his own play on that famous stage.

So, as the summer passes, Alexis writes his play for the next year's Festival. But then, with his friend Corinna, he learns that Athens has enemies – enemies who do not like Athenian democracy, and who are planning a revolution to end it all . . .

BOOKWORMS · CLASSICS · STAGE 3

Through the Looking-Glass

LEWIS CARROLL

Retold by Jennifer Bassett

'I wish I could get through into looking-glass house,' Alice said. 'Let's pretend that the glass has gone soft and . . . Why, I do believe it has! It's turning into a kind of cloud!'

A moment later Alice is inside the looking-glass world. There she finds herself part of a great game of chess, travelling through forests and jumping across brooks. The chess pieces talk and argue with her, give orders and repeat poems . . .

It is the strangest dream that anyone ever had . . .

BOOKWORMS · FANTASY & HORROR · STAGE 4

The Whispering Knights

PENELOPE LIVELY

Retold by Clare West

'I don't know that you have done anything wrong,' Miss Hepplewhite said. 'But it is possible that you have done something rather dangerous.'

William and Susie thought they were just playing a game when they cooked a witch's brew in the old barn and said a spell over it, but Martha was not so sure. And indeed, the three friends soon learn that they have called up something dark and evil out of the distant past . . .